I CHOOSE
To Be
HAPPY

CLYDE EMANUEL MCNELL

AuthorHouse™
1663 Liberty Drive
Bloomington, IN 47403
www.authorhouse.com
Phone: 833-262-8899

Because of the dynamic nature of the Internet, any web addresses or links contained in
this book may have changed since publication and may no longer be valid. The views
expressed in this work are solely those of the author and do not necessarily reflect the views
of the publisher, and the publisher hereby disclaims any responsibility for them.

This book is printed on acid-free paper.

ISBN: 978-1-6655-7559-1 (sc)
ISBN: 978-1-6655-7558-4 (e)

Library of Congress Control Number: 2022920964

Print information available on the last page.

Published by AuthorHouse   11/15/2022

authorHOUSE®

DEDICATION

I'm grateful that God has allowed me to write this book. May it bring all glory to Him. May it inspire and bless every reader.

I dedicate this book in memory of my parents The Late Pastor W. L. McNell, and Alma Wesley McNell who were God fearing dedicated servants of God.

My Gratitude

To my wife Denise, who serves in ministry with me by way of music ministry with all my love for 37 years of marriage:

To my son, Clyde "CJ" McNell Jr. of whom I love so much and who serves with me in ministry by way of music ministry:

To my son's wife and my daughter-in-love Mollie Rattler McNell,

and my grandson Jared Rattler, both who serve with me by way of music ministry:

To nephew Miquet Georgetown of whom I had the privilege of helping rear from age 13, who also serves with me by way of music ministry.

To all of my siblings living and deceased

To the congregations of which I pastor, New Light Baptist Church in Grosse Tete Louisiana and The Greater Pilgrim Rest Baptist Church in Plaquemine Louisiana.

To the people of Iberville Parish and surrounding areas.

Thank You!!!

FOREWORD

It is both an honor and privilege to exhort such a great read! "I Choose to Be Happy" has encouraged, inspired, and enhanced my life in so many ways. I thank God for Pastor C. E. McNell as he has written a true tool that readers can use to pattern as we make the daily choice to be happy in spite of what life may bring. This book not only gives personal testimony from the life of Pastor Mcnell but it is supported with scripture which is what we need to make the choice to be happy and his life's experience. Life can weigh us down sometimes but choosing to be happy in Christ makes the difference in how we handle what life may bring our way.

I'm forever grateful for the words written in this book along with the many years of teaching, preaching, and counsel my family and I have received from Pastor McNell that he has exemplified throughout this entire book. In his writing, Pastor Mcnell makes it plain and evident that although he is a man after God's own heart, like David, he has struggled with the choice to be happy as we all do struggle with this choice in our life. Pastor McNell referenced Psalm 55 being his go to scripture which from his teaching and counsel also became my go to scripture in life. Like Pastor McNell, I am so grateful that in my life, my Psalm 55 doesn't end the way that it begins because Jesus makes the difference.

This book was truly inspired by God's divine power laid on Pastor McNell's heart as he continues to teach, preach, and counsel throughout this writing with the spiritual well being of the body of Christ on his heart. I am eternally thankful to God that He thought enough of me to grace me with such a spiritual leader that continues to lead and guide many spiritually on this Christian journey. To God be the Glory as His Word continues to go forth through this book.

—Avis Williams

Spiritual sister, daughter, and friend in Jesus Christ

REJOICING

Philippians 4:4 Rejoice in the Lord always and again I say rejoice.

I use this scripture as an introduction to this book, because in this verse of scripture is a serious call to rejoice. The Apostle Paul, who wrote many of the books of the New Testament, says twice in the above verse that we are to rejoice. Because of the way the Apostle Paul emphasizes this command to rejoice as he does, indicates how serious of a matter it is to choose to rejoice. The word "always" certainly caught my eyes and caused me to think about this command. "Again I say unto you" is another emphasis to note and pay attention to. He really highlights this command.

Because of my desire to please God, I want to obey this command. Because I believe that blessings are a result of obedience, I want to obey this and any other command given to me in God's word. This is a command and not a suggestion to the one whose faith is in Jesus Christ. Truly my faith is in Jesus Christ.

We must never allow ourselves to see that which is written in the word of God as simply mere words on a page. Hebrews 4:12 says "For the word of God is quick, and powerful, and sharper than any twoedged sword, piercing even to the dividing asunder of soul and spirit, and of the joints and marrow, and is a discerner of the thoughts and intents of the heart." The Bible is a guide for living a life pleasing to God. The principles taught will bring joy to our lives. The Psalmist writes concerning God's word "Thy word is a lamp unto my feet, And a light unto my path." Psalm 119:105

When the seriousness of Philippians 4:4 is understood, along with other verses that contribute to it's importance we can conclude that we should choose to be happy. I will certainly share various bible verses that help support what Paul says to us about rejoicing.

Psalm 118 supports our position to choose to be happy. The psalmist says "This is the day which the LORD hath made; We will rejoice and be glad in it." Psalm 118:24 KJV. That sounds to me like someone making a choice to be happy. The psalmist made a choice to rejoice.

These words from the book of Philippians were penned by the apostle Paul from his prison stay in Rome or Ephesus. It seems ironic that he can teach others about how to have joy even though he was in prison when he wrote the letter. That gives this principle even more weight. He speaks from experience. Paul shares with his readers that which he has applied to his own life. Paul went through many trials in his life as a believer in Jesus Christ. He tells us in 2 Corinthians 11:24-27 "Of the Jews five times received I forty stripes save one. Thrice was I beaten with rods, once was I stoned, thrice I suffered shipwreck, a night and a day I have been in the deep; in journeyings often, in perils of waters, in perils of robbers, in perils by mine own countrymen, in perils by the heathen, in perils in the city, in perils in the wilderness, in perils in the sea, in perils among false brethren; in weariness and painfulness, in watchings often, in hunger and thirst, in fastings often, in cold and nakedness."

If the Apostle Paul could still maintain happiness after all of that, surely he is the right person to teach us how to have joy in spite of the perils of life.

Now I'm sure that the statement 'I choose to be happy' sounds easier said than done. This becomes a reality only as a result of an ever growing relationship with The Lord and Savior Jesus Christ. It only comes as a result of applying Biblical principles to our lives. In the biblical book of James in chapter 1:25 we are told that the blessed person is the one who applies biblical principles to his life. James puts it this way "But whoso looketh into the perfect law of liberty, and continueth therein, he being not a forgetful hearer, but a doer of the work, this man shall be blessed in his deed." This is why James tells us to be a doer of God's word and not a hearer only. Jesus Himself makes it plain that following His teachings ushers us into the blessings of God. In John 15:7 Jesus says "If ye abide in me, and my words abide in you, ye shall ask what ye will, and it shall be done unto you."

We must apply the principles taught in the word of God. In alcohol and drug programs there is a saying concerning the drug program that goes like this "It will work if you work it". I say the same about the word of God. It will work if you work it. Applying God's word consistently changes us for the better.

In order for this "choosing to be happy " to become a reality one must practice "choosing to be happy" consistently. You must make it a mental and spiritual practice in your life. My mother, the late Alma Wesley McNell, taught me a lesson that I shall never forget. She said "whatever you practice the most is what you will get down perfect. If you practice the wrong thing that's what you will get down perfect. If you practice the right thing, that's what you will get down perfect. What we must do is discontinue practices that will hurt us. We must practice that which will be a blessing to our lives. If we practice being mean we will get that down perfect. If we practice sadness we will get that down perfect. The old saying is practice makes perfect. May we strive to perfect the things that honor God.

When I use the statement 'I Choose To Be Happy', I am not trying to give the impression that I do not have burdens, trials and tribulations, because I like anyone else do have such. Applying God's word to my life and my circumstances is what allows me to have joy in the midst of burdens, trials and tribulations. I discovered some time ago that it is not what happens to us in life but it is how we respond to what happens to us, that makes the difference in whether we will still have joy. There was certainly a time when I would respond to situations in ways that did not glorify God. I would respond in anger and some rage. My mother had a talk with me one day concerning how I would respond to problems. I remember her words so well. She said Manuel, as I was sometimes called by family as I grew up, "You be in the right in the situations that you become angry about but you cut up so bad until you look wrong." She suggested that I calm down and respond in a way that doesn't make me look wrong. I remember the first time putting her advice into practice. It was in the early days of my pastorate of The New Light Baptist Church, of which I am presently pastor of. On my way to a meeting of the church, I said to myself that night that I would let others fuss and act inappropriately and when they finish I would calmly say the same thing that I normally would have said with rage, but now calmly. I was so proud of myself and knew that I had honored God in the way I handled the problem.

This is true of how we handle any trial or tribulation in our lives. We must respond to trials in a way that still honors God. The patriarch Job is a great example of someone who still honored God in spite of the tragedies in his life. He never lost faith in God. Job made this statement "Though he slay me, yet will I trust in him: But I will maintain mine own ways before him." Job 13:15 KJV

It is because of applying biblical principles to my life that I am able to maintain a degree of joy in my life. I have a favorite scripture that I call 'my life scripture'. Many who know me, (especially those of whom I serve as Pastor) know what my favorite scripture is, because I'm always sharing it in hopes of getting others to embrace it to help them move forward in this life. My favorite or life scripture is Philippians 3:13-14 "Brethren, I count not myself to have apprehended: but this one thing I do, forgetting those things which are behind, and reaching forth unto those things which are before, I press toward the mark for the prize of the high calling of God in Christ Jesus."

Living in the past will prevent one from experiencing joy. We can not return to the past . We cannot jump back to yesterday. We cannot live off of past failures nor past successes. We must also realize that we cannot spend our time worrying about tomorrow because there are no guarantees that tomorrow will come. I often say it this way, I can't jump back to yesterday and I cannot scoot up to tomorrow. All I have is today. God does not give us a week at a time nor does He give us a month at a time. He gives us one day at a time. In the book of Matthew we are told 'Sufficient unto the day is the evil thereof'. There is enough to deal with today rather than worrying about tomorrow.

To experience the joy of the Lord in my life and in choosing to be happy I forgive everyone who wrongs me and choose to hold no grudges towards anyone. Bitterness brings sadness. Even when others continue in their dislike of me, I realize that if I'm going to have the favor of God In my life that I must forgive those who wrong me. The Apostle Matthew records Jesus' words in Matthew 6:14-15 "For if ye forgive men their trespasses, your heavenly Father will also forgive you: but if ye forgive not men their trespasses, neither will your Father forgive your trespasses." In Psalm 66:**18 the psalmist says "**If I regard iniquity in my heart, the Lord will not hear me." I do not want my prayer life hung up because of any disobedience to God. I certainly want my prayers to be answered.

As I said before, being a doer of God's word makes all the difference. Loving people, forgiving people, showing people the love of God, are all things that we are called to do as believers in Christ Jesus. Our joy will come out of knowing that we are honoring God by doing these things. Doing these things brings joy.

Readers; please have no desire for your prayer life to be hindered because of regarding iniquity in your heart. This will cause you the opposite of happiness. The reason that I write this book is because I love seeing people happy. To hold a grudge against another is one having iniquity in his heart. In **James 5:9 we are told** "Grudge not one against another, brethren, lest ye be condemned." Refusing to forgive is regarding iniquity in one's heart. Not being kindly affectionate to one another is regarding iniquity in one's heart. The Apostle Paul says "and be ye kind one to another, tenderhearted, forgiving one another, even as God for Christ's sake hath forgiven you."Ephesians 4:32 KJV.

Let not jealousy envy or strife reside in the heart against another. Joy is found in knowing that your heart is free of these sins. Apply these principles and joy will be yours.

As I write this book I don't want anyone to think that I did not have to grow towards my present way of thinking. This is something that definitely calls for Spiritual growth. I have not always had or experienced this mindset concerning joy all of my life.

There was a time when many years ago Psalm 55 was a scripture that I frequented because it allowed me to express how I felt at a particular time in my life. It was at a time when I was dealing with sadness and depression in life over various circumstances and situations. This was a a time that I did not make the choice to be happy. It was at a time that I would so often find myself sad for any number of reasons. Psalm 55 begins with a sad and pitiful state expressed by King David. David writes in Psalm 55:1-8 "Give ear to my prayer, O God; And hide not thyself from my supplication. Attend unto me, and hear me: I mourn in my complaint, and make a noise; Because of the voice of the enemy, Because of the oppression of the wicked: For they cast iniquity upon me, And in wrath they hate me. My heart is sore pained within me: And the terrors of death are fallen upon me. Fearfulness and trembling are come upon me, And horror hath overwhelmed me. And I said, Oh that I had wings like a dove! For then would I fly away, and be at rest. Lo, then would I wander far off, And remain in the wilderness. Selah. I would hasten my escape From the windy storm and tempest."

This sounds like utter depression. As related to people in my life in those days, I embraced more words of Psalm 55 than perhaps any other scriptures. I certainly embraced the following words of Psalm 55 "For it was not an enemy that reproached me; Then I could have born it: Neither was it he that hated me that did magnify himself against me; Then I would have hid myself from him: But it was thou, a man mine equal, My guide, and mine acquaintance. We took sweet counsel together, And walked unto the house of God in company."Psalm 55:12-14 KJV.

We are often hurt most by those who seem to be closest to us. It is most likely the people closest to us whereby we are caught off guard by their behavior that ends up causing us sadness.

Always considering myself a true friend to people of whom I thought were genuinely my friends, I found myself so often hurt by those who smiled in my face as though they were my friends and were not. Those were depressing experiences. Dealing at times with family members whose love I yearned for but never felt were also times of depression and despondency. Dealing with ministry leaders who were less than loving and genuine in the faith, was also disappointing and a let down. Even though fake friends still exist. Even though still disliked by some family members, and even though still disliked by some ministry leaders, I choose today to be happy.

Know that in this life that the people who are going to love you are going to love you; and the ones that are not are not. but if they ever get saved they will love you too. That is the attitude that we must have.

I share all of this to express that it takes growth and a different mindset to get to a point where you can choose happiness in spite of the things that come our way that are designed by the enemy to make us sad. I choose to be happy becomes more than a saying or mere words to the one who grows in this Christian walk of life. The more we mature in Christ the more we are able to deal with sadness and depressing times in our lives. Every believer must strive to grow more and more mature so that he or she can experience more joy. An indication of immaturity is that of people who are always quarreling. People who are unable to get along with others because of contentions and bitterness in their hearts is a sign of spiritual immaturity. Paul writes. "And I, brethren, could not speak unto you as unto spiritual, but as unto carnal, even as unto babes in Christ. I have fed you with milk, and not with meat: for hitherto ye were not able to bear it, neither yet now are ye able. For ye are yet carnal: for whereas there is among you envying, and strife, and divisions, are ye not carnal, and walk as men?"
1 Corinthians 3:1-3 KJV

Spiritual growth must come intentionally. 2 Peter 2:18 commands us to grow in grace and in knowledge of our Lord and Savior Jesus Christ. Paul writes in Ephesians 4:14 "that we *henceforth* be no more children, tossed to and fro, and carried about with every wind of doctrine, by the sleight of men, *and*cunning craftiness, whereby they lie in wait to deceive; The best way to grow mature is through the study and application of God's word. Paul says "So then faith cometh by hearing, and hearing by the word of God." Romans 10:17 KJV. Constant exposure to the Word of God will grow your faith which will enable you to experience the joy of the Lord.

I feel that many people fail to live with joy because they have not learned to live in the moment. They have not learned to enjoy the moment. Oft time people are so focused on what is the next thing they will do and fail to enjoy the present moment. They fail to recognize the glory of God all around them. They fail to see His glory in the rising of the sun or in the going down of the same. They fail to see it in the cast of the rainbow. They fail to see His glory in blades of grass, or in the peaks of mountains. May we learn to enjoy the best of our surroundings no matter what they may be. Live in the moment. Whatever your present reality seems to be find joy there by focusing on Jesus, who is the author and finisher of our faith. Make the best of your present circumstances. Paul shares with us in Philippians "Not that I speak in respect of want: for I have learned, in whatsoever state I am, therewith to be content. I know both how to be abased, and I know how to abound: every where and in all things I am instructed both to be full and to be hungry, both to abound and to suffer need. I can do all things through Christ which strengtheneth me." Philippians 4:11-13 KJV

To have happiness or joy in all circumstances, one must receive help and strength from Christ.

We live with so much anxiety in this world. So many people seem to be always on the edge. So many people seem extremely frustrated with life. So many are ready to throw in the towel and quit life. We are commanded in Philippians 4:6 to be anxious for nothing. What is the best way to get rid of our anxiety? The answer lies in that same verse, Philippians 4:6, where we are told to make our request known unto God. We must believe that praying to God about any situation in our lives is truly going to affect the outcome of the situation. It will affect the outcome for the better . Paul writes in Philippians 4:6 "Be careful for nothing; but in every thing by prayer and supplication with thanksgiving let your requests be made known unto God." That is the attitude that the

Bible teaches us to have in life. Take everything that causes us to be filled with anxiety to God. If we do what verse 6 says, what we are told in verse 7 will be our result. Verse 7 says "And the peace of God, which passeth all understanding, shall keep your hearts and minds through Christ Jesus." If we practice doing verse 6, we will end up with peace that surpasses all understanding. We will not lose heart nor mind.

I believe that to a great extent that people who pray often is a sign of their faith. Going to God in prayer shows faith in Him. You don't generally go to someone who you don't think can help you. You go to God because you believe that He can do something about your situation. A lack of a consistent and persistent prayer life seems like a lack of faith in the Lord.

The key to getting your problems fixed is to ask God to fix them. James tells us "Ye lust, and have not: ye kill, and desire to have, and cannot obtain: ye fight and war, yet ye have not, because ye ask not."
James 4:2 KJV

Jesus makes a statement that when you give it proper thought, you conclude that the statement is simple. I think many miss the power of the statement and the accompanying explanation that comes with it. The statement is so simple. He makes it a no brainer if you are a believer. He says "ask and it shall be given". This is really talking about praying. Here I share His entire logic about this statement. "Ask, and it shall be given you; seek, and ye shall find; knock, and it shall be opened unto you: for every one that asketh receiveth; and he that seeketh findeth; and to him that knocketh it shall be opened. Or what man is there of you, whom if his son ask bread, will he give him a stone? Or if he ask a fish, will he give him a serpent? If ye then, being evil, know how to give good gifts unto your children, how much more shall your Father which is in heaven give good things to them that ask him?"Matthew 7:7-11 KJV

The idea is that our God loves us and truly wants what is best for us. He must not be pictured as a mean uncaring person who is waiting for our downfall. That is not who He is. Remember how much God loves us. Remember John 3:16 "For God so loved the world, that he gave his only begotten Son, that whosoever believeth in him should not perish, but have everlasting life."

Practice asking this loving God, who is Father to every person who has trusted His son for salvation for what you want. Let praying to God be a practice in your life. 1 Thessalonians 5:17 says "Pray without ceasing." Learn to pray little sporadic prayers throughout the day. You don't have to wait until you have opportunity to kneel down on the floor. The position of your body is not what is important in praying. The position of your heart is what is important.

Don't wait for bedtime to pray. The devil is busy all day and people are often being used by him to harm you. For that reason you need to heed 1 Thessalonians 5:17. Those sporadic prayers throughout the day keeps you in touch with God the Father. It also helps you to grow an intimacy with our God.

Some people teach that you should pray about something one time and then leave it alone and never pray about it again. That is not what the Bible teaches. Jesus tells us in Luke 18 that we ought to always pray and never give up. We are taught in Luke 18 the importance of being persistent in our prayer life. Luke writes "And he spake a parable unto them to this end, that men ought always to pray, and not to faint; saying, There was in a city a judge, which feared not God, neither regarded man: and there was a widow in that city; and she came unto him, saying, Avenge me of mine adversary. And he would not for a while: but afterward he said within himself, Though I fear not God, nor regard man; yet because this widow troubleth me, I will avenge her, lest by her continual coming she weary me. And the Lord said, Hear what the unjust judge saith. And shall not God avenge his own elect, which cry day and night unto him, though he bear long with them?"
Luke 18:1-7 KJV

Praying about something more than once is acceptable to God. Paul is an example of such. Paul shares "And lest I should be exalted above measure through the abundance of the revelations, there was given to me a thorn in the flesh, the messenger of Satan to buffet me, lest I should be exalted above measure. For this thing I besought the Lord thrice, that it might depart from me. And he said unto me, My grace is sufficient for thee: for my strength is made perfect in weakness. Most gladly therefore will I rather glory in my infirmities, that the power of Christ may rest upon me." 2 Corinthians 12:7-9 KJV. He says he prayed about it three times before God told him that His grace was sufficient for him.

The ultimate example of praying consistently about something until you get your answer is Jesus. The night before His crucifixion, Jesus prayed in the Garden of Gethsemane. Each time He came back to check on the disciples, He would return back to His prayer session. Mark records for us concerning this event "And again he went away, and prayed, and spake the same words." Mark 14:39 KJV

If we are going to choose to be happy in this life we have to choose to not be a vengeful person. We must trust God enough to know that it is not necessary to seek our own vengeance on those who have wronged us. I tell people all the time; I'm not going to have God to have to whip you and me. If you do me wrong I'm not going to try to get you back because God is already going to deal with you for doing me wrong but if I get my own revenge that means I'm taking His place. If I take His place he then owes me a chastising. The best way to please God is to treat everyone the way we are supposed to treat them. Treat everyone with godly love. That means even those who have wronged us.

I determined years ago that my happiness in life would not be dependent upon any one or more individuals. If I focus on the salvation acquired for me by the death of Jesus Christ, I believe I can overcome every ill intended thing done to me by anyone.

I'm a person who does not like drama and chaos and to choose to be happy I embrace a mindset that allows some distance spiritually and mentally between chaos and myself. I do realize that it is impossible to avoid drama of life completely. I trust God for biblical principles on conflict resolution. I choose to occupy my mind with what the Apostles Paul commands in Philippians 4:8 "Finally, brethren, whatsoever things are true, whatsoever things are honest, whatsoever things are just, whatsoever things are pure, whatsoever things are lovely, whatsoever things are of good report; if there be any virtue, and if there be any praise, think on these things." I have learned the importance of renewal of mind as stated by the Apostle Paul in Romans 12:2 "And be not conformed to this world: but be ye transformed by the renewing of your mind, that ye may prove what is that good, and acceptable, and perfect, will of God."

Choosing to be happy calls for making mental and spiritual adjustments. Sometimes it calls for making physical adjustments as well. If a particular thing is causing me sorrow and pain at any given time I pray about it. If necessary I find something else to do that will bring me relief. When I need to I have my cry and Pray some more about the circumstance and focus on honoring God by doing whatever it is that I believe honors Him.

Something as simple as getting away from the circumstance that is causing the pain often works in moving forward in joy. I'm not advocating that we run away from our problems but I am saying that we must not overly indulge ourselves to the extent that we stress ourselves out over the matter. Sometimes you have to decide to leave the problem alone for now and return to it with a clearer mind later. Be careful with making decisions based on impulse or on mere emotions. Make decisions based off of looking at the big picture. Think about whether or not the decision that you are making will cause more chaos or will it bring peace. The Bible tells us to pursue peace. "Depart from evil, and do good; Seek peace, and pursue it."
Psalm 34:14 KJV

Learn to recognize and enjoy the people that God has placed in your lives. Every gift is not wrapped in gift wrap paper. The people whom God places in our lives are great and wonderful gifts within themselves. It is often times that without even knowing that you are burdened that anyone of those people will show up with a call or a visit at just the right time. Let those people know that you appreciate them.

Focus on bringing joy into the lives of others and see how much doing that will bring joy into your life. Have the attitude of the apostle Paul who realized that each of us can pour into each other's lives. "For I long to see you, that I may impart unto you some spiritual gift, to the end ye may be established; that is, that I may be comforted together with you by the mutual faith both of you and me."
Romans 1:11-12 KJV

I have so wanted to write this book for a long time but for whatever reason I am just now committing myself or returning to this task. What I had sometimes called procrastination, could have been the need for me to experience more sad moments that could challenge me in my title of this book. This title sounds good but it goes without saying that Choosing to be happy is not easy. But I say I again as I have stated earlier that with applying biblical principles it is possible.

I have experience the many highs and lows of life but God has always brought me through. I can rejoice because my God's track record is excellent. Knowing that sooner or later He is going to fix whatever problems that exist in my life gives me great satisfaction.

Now this calls for patience. Patience in God also calls for Trusting God. King David said "I waited patiently for the LORD; And he inclined unto me, and heard my cry. He brought me up also out of an horrible pit, out of the miry clay, And set my feet upon a rock, and established my goings. And he hath put a new song in my mouth, even praise unto our God: Many shall see it, and fear, And shall trust in the LORD." Psalm 40:1-3 KJV

The result of patience is joy in God.

It is my greatest desire, that those who read this book will apply the biblical principles that I have shared. The book is a somewhat short synopsis of the way that I operate in my life. It is a look into my heart. It reveals my way of thinking. I try my best to think biblically as I move through life and as I counsel others seeking their joy for life as well.